A TRUE BOOK™

Incredible Plants!

Plant Life Cycles

Mara Grunbaum

Children's Press®
An Imprint of Scholastic Inc.

Content Consultant
Michael Freeling, PhD
Professor
Department of Plant & Microbial Biology
University of California, Berkeley
Berkeley, California

Library of Congress Cataloging-in-Publication Data
Title: Plant life cycles / by Mara Grunbaum.
Description: New York, NY : Children's Press, an imprint of Scholastic Inc., 2020. | Series: A true book |
    Includes bibliographical references and index.
Identifiers: LCCN 2019004805 | ISBN 9780531234655 (library binding) | ISBN 9780531240083
    (paperback)
Subjects: LCSH: Plants—Life cycles—Juvenile literature.
Classification: LCC QK49 .G735 2020 | DDC 581—dc23
LC record available at https://lccn.loc.gov/2019004805

All rights reserved. Published in 2020 by Children's Press, an imprint of Scholastic Inc.
Printed in Heshan, China 62

SCHOLASTIC, CHILDREN'S PRESS, A TRUE BOOK™, and associated logos are trademarks and/or
registered trademarks of Scholastic Inc.

Scholastic Inc., 557 Broadway, New York, NY 10012

1 2 3 4 5 6 7 8 9 10 R 29 28 27 26 25 24 23 22 21 20

**Front cover: Young plants at
different stages of growth**

**Back cover: Garden balsam plant
shooting out seeds**

Find the Truth!

Everything you are about to read is true *except* for one of the sentences on this page.

Which one is **TRUE**?

T or F Some plants spread their seeds through animal droppings.

T or F A tree's leaves turn red when they've absorbed too much sunlight.

Find the answers in this book.

Contents

A tree among wildflowers

Avocados

The **BIG** Truth

Other Ways to Grow

Ginger

Think About It!

Look closely at the photo on these pages. What do you think you see? Is there an animal? A plant? How are they interacting? Why do you think this is happening? What evidence in the photo supports your ideas?

Intrigued?
Want to know more? Turn the page!

Nectar from flowers gives this hawk moth energy to stay alive.

If you guessed that the photo shows an insect covered in pollen, you are right! The insect on page 6 is called a hawk moth. It uses its curly, straw-like tongue to sip nectar from flowers. Tiny yellow grains of pollen stick to the insect's body as it feeds.

Why is the moth there? The plant's colorful flowers and sweet nectar attracted the moth. The plant benefits when such visitors carry its pollen away.

Some plants spread pollen as part of their life cycle. This is the process by which organisms grow and reproduce over their lives. There are many different types of plants, from fuzzy mosses to towering trees. Some flower; others do not. Yet almost all of them have something in common: They use sunlight to make their own food. In this book, you'll learn how plants do this and how they spread and thrive.

This tree and the flowers surrounding it are all plants.

This scientist climbs up giant sequoia trees to study them.

Sequoias have thick bark that protects them from forest fires. The trees can live 3,000 years!

1

Starting Small

In a forest in Northern California, a team of scientists wake up early. They strap on helmets and climbing harnesses and fasten themselves to ropes. Then they start climbing the trunks of giant sequoia trees. These plants are some of the tallest trees in the world. Giant sequoias can grow nearly 300 feet (91 meters) high. That's as tall as a 30-story building! But the sequoias began their lives like most plants do: as tiny seeds.

Spores and Seeds

Plants such as mosses, ferns, and horsetails can get their start as **spores**. A spore is just one cell surrounded by a protective outer coat. Most spores are so small you need a microscope to see them. All other plants begin as seeds. Seeds are bigger than spores, but they're much smaller than the plants they grow into. The seed of a giant sequoia tree is no larger than a grain of oatmeal.

Inside a Seed

A seed contains the ingredients that a new plant needs to start growing. In the middle of the seed is the baby plant, called the embryo. It's surrounded by the endosperm. This is a starchy material that provides food for the embryo. A tough seed coat surrounds the embryo and endosperm. It protects the new plant until it is ready to **germinate**, or sprout.

This diagram shows the basic parts of a seed.

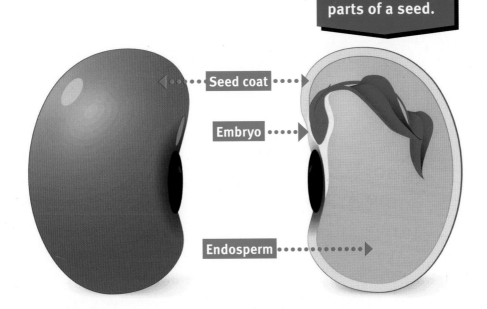

Seed coat

Embryo

Endosperm

What Seeds Need

A seed's coat seals in moisture. This keeps the embryo alive in a **dormant**, or resting, state. Some seeds stay dormant for only a few days before sprouting. Others can sprout after thousands of years! A seed needs three things to start growing: warmth, moisture, and oxygen. A seed planted in winter stays dormant until temperatures rise in spring. Over time, cracks form in the seed coat. This lets in water and oxygen-rich air.

Gardeners soak or scratch some seeds so the plants sprout more easily.

Gardeners space out seeds so each one has room to grow.

As a seed germinates, roots grow down and shoots grow up.

Breaking Out

As water seeps in, the seed swells. It bursts through whatever is left of the seed coat. The root, which grows downward out of the seed, is the first part of the plant to start growing. It anchors the seedling and begins soaking up water and nutrients from the soil. After that, a shoot grows upward. It unfurls to reveal one or two tiny leaves, the first of many the plant will make.

A single bamboo plant can have many offshoots.

Some bamboo species can grow more than 1 inch (2.5 centimeters) per hour!

Powering Up

Unlike animals, plants grow their whole lives. That's true whether they live for a few months or hundreds of years. One bristlecone pine tree in California is more than 5,000 years old, and it's been growing slowly the whole time! Growing continuously takes a lot of energy. Animals gather energy by eating, which most plants cannot do. Instead, plants are built to collect the energy they need from the sun.

Food Factories

Plant leaves are green because they contain a green pigment called chlorophyll. Chlorophyll's color allows it to absorb energy from sunlight and transfer it into the plant. Plant cells use this energy to power a chemical process that makes food for the plant. It creates oxygen for the atmosphere, and food for other organisms, as well. This process is called **photosynthesis**, a combination of Greek words that means "building from light."

Large leaves help a plant soak up light.

Sunlight isn't the only ingredient in photosynthesis. Plants also need water and nutrients from the ground and carbon dioxide from the air. During photosynthesis, plant cells break down the water and carbon dioxide. They use the components to make oxygen and sugars. The oxygen is released back into the air. The sugars are combined into more complex substances, which are used to build every part of the growing plant.

Light energy

Oxygen

Carbon dioxide

Minerals

Water

This diagram shows what plants take in and release during photosynthesis.

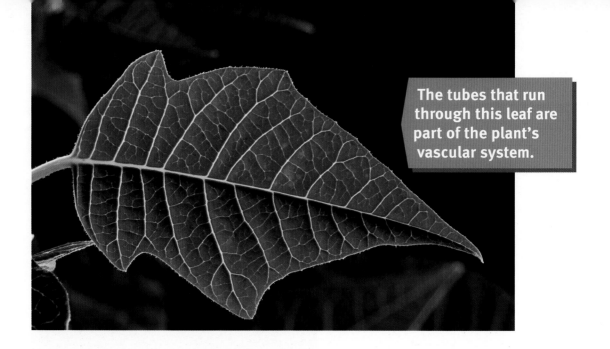

The tubes that run through this leaf are part of the plant's vascular system.

Transport System

Plants need to circulate water and nutrients through their entire bodies. As they grow, many plants form a network of tubes to do this. One set of tubes carries water from the plant's roots up to its leaves and branches. Another set carries sugars from the leaves to the rest of the plant. This system allows **vascular** plants to grow taller than nonvascular plants such as mosses, which must stay close to the damp ground.

Fall Leaves

In winter, there isn't much sunlight to give plants energy. Some trees, called deciduous trees, drop their leaves instead of using up precious energy to keep them alive. But before the leaves fall, the trees pull water and nutrients out of them. They break down chlorophyll and store it up to recycle the next year. Without the green chlorophyll, other pigments in the leaves become visible. Many of these pigments are stunning shades of yellow, orange, or red. Plants that retain their leaves through the year are called evergreen.

Deciduous forests turn a variety of colors in the fall.

Flowers cover a meadow in the mountains of Washington State.

All plants have ways to reproduce both sexually and asexually. The methods they use depend on what type of plant they are.

Becoming Plant Parents

Once they have matured, plants can reproduce. To do this, they must pass on copies of their **DNA**. DNA contains the instructions for making an organism. Every living cell has a copy of the organism's DNA inside. All plants have two ways of reproducing: sexually and asexually. Sexual reproduction is when two organisms combine their DNA into one cell that grows into a new individual. In asexual reproduction, an organism copies its own DNA.

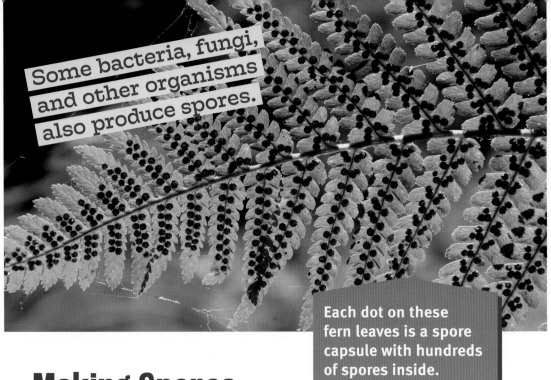

Some bacteria, fungi, and other organisms also produce spores.

Each dot on these fern leaves is a spore capsule with hundreds of spores inside.

Making Spores

Mosses, horsetails, and ferns are seedless plants. One way they reproduce is with spores. For example, some of the leaves on a fern produce clusters of tiny brown spore capsules. Inside each capsule, cells divide asexually to form hundreds of individual spores. When the capsules dry out, they burst open and millions of spores emerge. The spores drift on the wind or in water to find a new place to grow.

If a spore finds a suitable landing spot, it starts to develop. It grows into a form of the plant that reproduces sexually. In ferns, this form is called the prothallium. It is less than 0.3 inches (8 millimeters) across, no longer than a grain of rice. It is shaped like a tiny heart and lies flat on the ground. It produces male (sperm) and female (egg) cells that combine, and the DNA inside these cells combine as well. This makes a new baby fern.

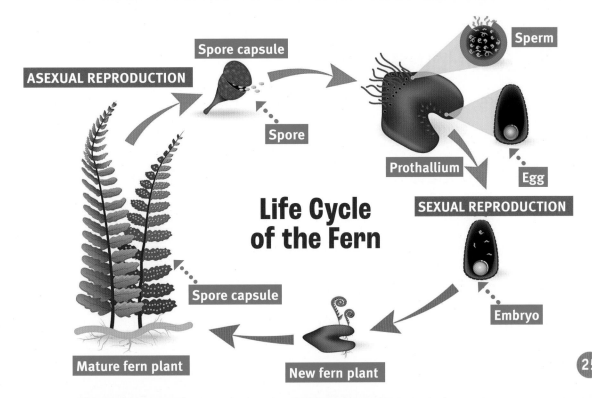

Life Cycle of the Fern

ASEXUAL REPRODUCTION

Spore capsule

Spore

Sperm

Prothallium

Egg

SEXUAL REPRODUCTION

Embryo

Spore capsule

Mature fern plant

New fern plant

Pollen Production

Conifers, such as pine and hemlock trees, sexually reproduce using structures called cones. Conifers have both male and female cones. Usually, both are found on the same tree. In spring, male cones produce millions of tiny pollen grains. Each one contains a copy of half of the tree's DNA. As the cones dry out, they release the pollen into the wind.

Achoo!

Do you ever become sniffly when you go outside in springtime? Eight percent of kids have hay fever, an allergic reaction to something in the air. In most cases, the culprit is pollen released by plants trying to reproduce! Pollen floating in the air drifts into a person's mouth and nostrils. Allergies happen when the person's body overreacts to these invaders. It sniffles and sneezes to try and expel the pollen. Bless you!

Pollen grains are microscopic. If enlarged, they could look something like this.

In Full Bloom

Most plants in the world make flowers for sexual reproduction. Many flowers contain both male and female parts. The male parts, called **stamens**, make pollen. To spread it, flowers attract animals such as bees, moths, bats, and hummingbirds. Bright colors tell a bee that the flower has nectar inside it. When it lands on the flower to feed, pollen sticks to its body. When the bee moves to a new flower, it carries pollen along.

Bees pollinate many food crops, including apples and broccoli.

A Seed Forms

When a pollen grain lands on a female part of a flower, called the pistil, it joins with the **ovule** inside. Inside the ovule are two special cells: an egg and a similar, egg-like cell. The pollen **fertilizes** these two special cells. The fertilized egg goes on to make an embryo for a new plant. The other, egg-like cell becomes the seed around the embryo.

This diagram shows the life stages of a typical flowering plant.

Other Ways to Grow

Plants do not always need flowers, cones, or spores to reproduce. Many plants can also reproduce asexually with a method called vegetative reproduction. Here are a few examples of how that happens.

Rhizomes

Rhizomes are stems that grow horizontally underground. New roots and shoots grow from them.

Plants that use this method: Bamboo, ginger

Ginger

Runners

Runners are stems that grow out along the ground's surface. New roots and shoots grow from points along them called nodes.

Plants that use this method: Strawberries

Strawberries

Tubers and Taproots

Tubers are swollen stem parts. Taproots are swollen root parts. Both store a plant's nutrients and can produce new plants.

Plants that use this method:
Potatoes, parsnips

Potatoes

Bulbs and Corms

Bulbs and corms are swollen parts that grow at the base of the parent plant. Each one can sprout into a new plant.

Plants that use this method:
Onions, crocuses

Crocuses

And more!

Other plants, such as spider plants, can produce new roots and leaves from leaf edges. Mosses and liverworts can grow new plants from pieces that have been separated from the original plant.

Spider plant

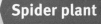

31

A single dandelion plant produces thousands of seeds.

Seeds that drift on the wind help dandelions spread.

4

A New Home

Have you ever blown the seeds off a dandelion? If so, you were helping its life cycle along. Seeds and spores need to travel away from their parent plants so they don't compete with one another for light, water, and nutrients. Blowing on the wind is one way they can **disperse**. Dandelion seeds are shaped like tiny umbrellas, which helps them float farther. They can drift more than 325 feet (100 m)!

Catching a Wave

Seeds and spores can also travel by water. The coconut palm, which grows naturally on beaches, drops its seeds directly into the sea. Coconuts can drift for many miles in the ocean while the seed stays dormant. Air pockets inside a coconut help it float. The seed germinates once it washes up on a new beach. Scientists think that floating helped coconuts spread to tropical shores around the world over thousands of years.

Parts of the coconut plant can be used as food, drink, fiber, and more.

A coconut grows roots and shoots only after washing ashore.

Tiny hooks help some seeds hitch rides on hairy animals.

Hitching a Ride

Some plants count on animals to spread their seeds for them. A plant called the burdock, for instance, grows seeds covered in tiny, Velcro-like hooks. When a furry animal brushes past the burdock, the spiky burrs catch in its fur. Later, when the animal finally rubs the burrs off, the seeds fall to the ground and grow in a new place.

Orangutans help replant the forest by eating fruits and dropping the seeds in their dung.

Eat Me!

Other seeds also travel with animals—not on the outside of their bodies, but inside! Many flowering plants surround their seeds with fleshy fruit or sweet berries. This attracts animals to eat the fruits, along with the seeds inside. As an animal digests the fruit, the seeds start to break open. Eventually, the seeds come out in the animal's droppings. The droppings give seeds an extra boost of nutrients as they start to grow.

Super Seed

Why do avocados have enormous seeds? Because they used to be spread by enormous animals! Sixty-five million years ago, huge North American mammals such as mammoths and giant ground sloths ate whole avocados. They were the only animals big enough to digest the pits and spread them in their dung. These giant mammals became extinct about 13,000 years ago. Since then, avocados can only grow if human farmers plant their seeds.

A touch-me-not plant bursts open to fling out its seeds.

Exploding Away

A few plants grow seedpods that explode and fling seeds away from the plant. Witch hazel plants, for example, produce woody capsules with two seeds inside. The seeds take a full year to mature. When the capsules dry out the next autumn, they burst open with a loud pop. This launches the seeds up to 20 feet (6 m) away!

Life After Death

Some plants, such as sunflowers, live for less than a year. They germinate in spring, bloom in summer, and die after scattering seeds in fall. Trees can live for decades or even centuries and reproduce many times. And a dead plant can still help other plants and animals. As soon as it dies, it starts to decompose, or break down.

Fallen trees still provide shelter and food to other organisms.

Young plants grow from the rotting stump of a fallen tree.

Mold and other tiny organisms kick off the decomposition process by eating nutrients from the dead plant. Next, small animals such as millipedes and earthworms gradually break the plant down into soil. A large tree can take many years to rot completely, dropping limbs over a long period of time. The rotting wood provides a warm, wet home where new seedlings can sprout. Some of them may be descendants of the dead plant, growing from seeds that fell close to the tree.

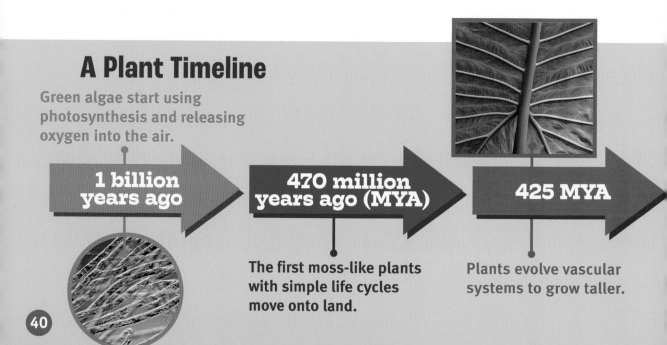

A Plant Timeline

Green algae start using photosynthesis and releasing oxygen into the air.

1 billion years ago

470 million years ago (MYA)

425 MYA

The first moss-like plants with simple life cycles move onto land.

Plants evolve vascular systems to grow taller.

Branching Out

When plants reproduce sexually, the new plants have different DNA from each of their parents. That means they can have slightly different traits than their parent plants did. Over many generations, this helps plants develop new forms and survival strategies. As a result, they can adjust to different climates and habitats. Over millions of years, small changes add up to big ones. They can lead to entirely new types of plants with their own ways to live and grow.

The first seed-producing plants start to grow.

There are about 400,000 known species of plants.

300 MYA

200 MYA

Today

Plants start evolving flowers to help them reproduce.

Make a Seed Sprout!

In this activity, you will learn more about how plants germinate.

Materials

- 4 paper towels
- 4 zip-top sandwich bags
- Spray bottle with water
- 4 dry pinto beans

Directions

1 Fold each paper towel so it will fit in a sandwich bag. Use the spray bottle to moisten two of the paper towels. Leave the other two dry.

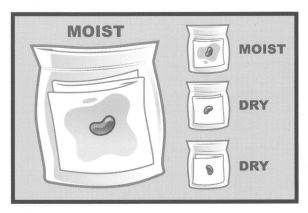

2 Slide each paper towel into a bag so it lays flat. Place a pinto bean on top of each paper towel. Seal the bags.

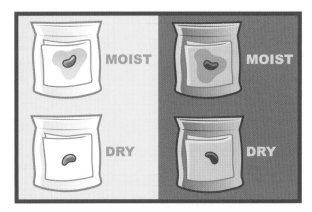

3 Put one moist bag and one dry bag in a warm, sunny spot, such as a windowsill. Put the other two bags in a cold, dark place, like the back of a cabinet.

4 Check each bag after three, five, and seven days. What has happened? Did any of the seeds sprout?

Explain It!

Using what you learned in this book, can you explain what happened to each pinto bean? If you need help, turn back to page 14 for more information.

True Statistics

Age of the oldest dormant seeds that scientists have successfully germinated: 32,000 years

Distance a bamboo plant can grow upward per day: 35 in. (89 cm)

Maximum width of a rafflesia flower, the largest in the world: 3 ft. (1 m)

Average number of seeds produced by one dandelion flower: 175

Approximate number of new plant species identified each year: 2,000

Weight of the largest fruit ever grown, a pumpkin: 2,624 lb. (1,190 kg)

Age of the oldest confirmed individual plant, a bristlecone pine in California: 5,062 years

Did you find the truth?

T Some plants spread their seeds through animal droppings.

F A tree's leaves turn red when they've absorbed too much sunlight.

Resources

Other books in this series:

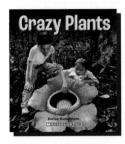

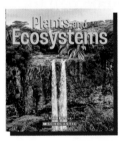

You can also look at:

Bang, Molly, and Penny Chisholm. *Ocean Sunlight: How Tiny Plants Feed the Seas*. New York: Blue Sky Press, 2012.

Burnie, David. *Plant*. London: DK Publishing, 2011.

Cornell, Kari. *Dig In: 12 Easy Gardening Projects Using Kitchen Scraps*. Minneapolis: Millbrook Press, 2018.

Dorion, Christiane. *How Plants and Trees Work: A Hands-on Guide to the Natural World*. Somerville, MA: Candlewick Press, 2017.

Willis, Kathy. *Botanicum*. Somerville, MA: BPP, 2017.

Glossary

conifers (KAHN-uh-fuhrz) trees or shrubs that produce their seeds in cones

disperse (dis-PUHRS) to spread widely from one original source

DNA (DEE-EN-AY) the material in genes that passes traits from one generation to the next

dormant (DOR-muhnt) in a temporary state of inactivity

fertilizes (FUR-tuh-lize-iz) joins a male and female cell to form a new individual

germinate (JUR-muh-nayt) to sprout as a seed or spore

ovule (AHV-yool) the part of the mother plant that forms a seed after fertilization

photosynthesis (foh-toh-SIN-thuh-sus) the process by which plant cells use energy from the sun to combine water, carbon dioxide, and minerals to make food

spores (SPORZ) plant cells that develop into a new plant

stamens (STAY-muhnz) the male parts of flowers that produce pollen

vascular (VAS-kyuh-lur) having tubelike vessels in the body to transport water and other liquids

Index

Page numbers in **bold** indicate illustrations.

About the Author

Mara Grunbaum is an award-winning science writer for children and adults. She's the former editor of *SuperScience*, Scholastic's science magazine for students in elementary school. She's written about everything from giant sinkholes to the physics of roller coasters, but she's most fascinated by living things like plants and animals. She lives in Seattle, Washington, with a growing collection of houseplants and one weird cat.